YOUR KNOWLEDGE HAS VALUE

- We will publish your bachelor's and
  master's thesis, essays and papers

- Your own eBook and book -
  sold worldwide in all relevant shops

- Earn money with each sale

Upload your text at www.GRIN.com
and publish for free

Lea Lorena Jerns

An analysis of Ambrose Bierce's "An Occurrence at Owl Creek Bridge"

GRIN Verlag

Bibliografische Information der Deutschen Nationalbibliothek:

Die Deutsche Bibliothek verzeichnet diese Publikation in der Deutschen National-
bibliografie; detaillierte bibliografische Daten sind im Internet über http://dnb.d-
nb.de/ abrufbar.

Dieses Werk sowie alle darin enthaltenen einzelnen Beiträge und Abbildungen
sind urheberrechtlich geschützt. Jede Verwertung, die nicht ausdrücklich vom
Urheberrechtsschutz zugelassen ist, bedarf der vorherigen Zustimmung des Verla-
ges. Das gilt insbesondere für Vervielfältigungen, Bearbeitungen, Übersetzungen,
Mikroverfilmungen, Auswertungen durch Datenbanken und für die Einspeicherung
und Verarbeitung in elektronische Systeme. Alle Rechte, auch die des auszugsweisen
Nachdrucks, der fotomechanischen Wiedergabe (einschließlich Mikrokopie) sowie
der Auswertung durch Datenbanken oder ähnliche Einrichtungen, vorbehalten.

Imprint:

Copyright © 2011 GRIN Verlag GmbH
Druck und Bindung: Books on Demand GmbH, Norderstedt Germany
ISBN: 978-3-656-72525-1

GRIN - Your knowledge has value

Der GRIN Verlag publiziert seit 1998 wissenschaftliche Arbeiten von Studenten, Hochschullehrern und anderen Akademikern als eBook und gedrucktes Buch. Die Verlagswebsite www.grin.com ist die ideale Plattform zur Veröffentlichung von Hausarbeiten, Abschlussarbeiten, wissenschaftlichen Aufsätzen, Dissertationen und Fachbüchern.

Visit us on the internet:

http://www.grin.com/

http://www.facebook.com/grincom

http://www.twitter.com/grin_com

Universität Potsdam

Institut für Anglistik/Amerikanistik

Midterm Assignment

Wintersemester 2010/2011

Abgabe bis: 27.01.2012

Lea Lorena Jerns

05.01.2012

Midterm Assignment

An Occurrence at Owl Creek Bridge

1. Ambrose Bierce's short story "An Occurrence at Owl Creek Bridge" is divided into three sections. In part I as well as in part II the story is told by an authorial narrator, which is also called heterodiegetic narrator. He tells us the short story from a perspective that enables the reader to look at the characters' world from the outside. The authorial narrator is omniscient, so he has an unlimited point of view and has the ability to look into characters but cannot share their world (non-identity). That means, he is not a character in the story himself. We can also speak of a dominant narrator, also called external focalizer, in these parts of the story mentioned above, as the external focalization "presents information of characters' external behavior (…)." (Michael Meyer 82). The authorial narrator also uses words like "he or "she" and not "I'.

The narrator is fairly reliable as he is omniscient and therefore "can expose secrets that characters hide from each other or those that are hidden from themselves with the effect that the reader gains an insight into hypocrisy and blindness." (Michael Meyer 74).

In part III there is a figural narrative situation because the reader gets "the impression that he could share the thoughts, feelings and perceptions of the character" (Michael Meyer 74) that is, with regard to this story, Peyton Farquhar. Thus, it is also obvious that we can speak of a dominant reflector, also called internal or character focalizer. Due to the figural narrative situation and the limited point of view the reader knows about the characters' thoughts and feelings etc., but is not able to know everything or to enter everybody's mind as he could if we would speak of an authorial narrator.

In the last sentence of part III the narrator becomes an authorial omniscient narrator with an unlimited point of view that tells us that the character Peyton Farquhar,

Universität Potsdam

Institut für Anglistik/Amerikanistik

Midterm Assignment

Wintersemester 2010/2011

Abgabe bis: 27.01.2012

Lea Lorena Jerns

05.01.2012

with whom we lived through just about all his adventures, never experienced these adventures because he has already died.

Finally, the narrator is less reliable because of the fact that until the end of the story everything seems like realism but in the end it is anything but realism. This blend of realism lets the reader call into question the reliability of the narrator.

2. The story's effect on the reader is a very surprising effect, especially because of the unexpected ending of the story. When it turns out that all of the long events and descriptions only took place in a very short time in Farquhar's head just before dying and did never happen in reality the reader is totally surprised, irritated and shocked at the same time. Thus Ambrose Bierce manipulated the reader by using the imaginations of the main character. This character is so strong developed, that the reader trusts him and follows his tracks without having any doubts with regard to his credibility. But, however, Peyton Farquhar gets diverted by his own thoughts and so the plot drags out in all kinds of unorganized directions. So the story is absolutely unpredictable till the end and this is what makes the story so astoundingly.

If the use of narrative situations would have been changed, the effect on the reader would have been totally different, especially in part III in which, except in the last sentence, the figural narrative situation is used to lead the reader through the story. If the figural narrative situation had been replaced by an authorial narrator the reader would have been aware, from the beginning, of the fact that everything that apparently happened is not reality but just happened in Farquhar's head because of the omniscient narrator and thus, there would not have been any surprising and at the same time confusing effect on the reader in the end.

But it would have been possible to tell the story by using a first-person narrator who experience all those adventures in the river, in the forest etc. and thus let the reader believe that everything that happens is real, because the authorial narrator discloses the secret not before the last sentence.

Universität Potsdam   05.01.2012

Institut für Anglistik/Amerikanistik

Midterm Assignment

Wintersemester 2010/2011

Abgabe bis: 27.01.2012

Lea Lorena Jerns

3. The story takes place during the American Civil War at Owl Creek Bridge which
   is in Alabama. At the beginning of the story the protagonist Peyton Farquhar, a
   Confederate sympathizer, stands bound at the bridge's edge condemned to death
   by hanging from Owl Creek Bridge due to his plan to burn down this bridge when
   a gray-clad soldier, who was actually a Federal scout, enlisted him to sabotage the
   bridge.

   There are also settings that only appear in the protagonist's imagination as for example in part III when Farquhar found himself in the river after the rope had bro-
   ken and afterwards in the forest, on the roadway and finally nearby his home.

4. Time is one of the most significant markers in this short story to let the reader
   know what is happening and how it should be perceived. Things are described
   very detailed in many words, sentences or even paragraphs are used to relate a sin-
   gle second. So the time itself in the story is not real but surreal and is only perceived by the characters and readers to be real. That means that the ratio between
   story time and discourse time differ widely from each other.

   We learn about that for example in part I of the story in paragraph five when Farquhar perceives respectively experiences the ticking of his watch that slow and
   clear that it appears to him like the ringing of a knell.

   Another example would be in part III when the reader experiences the imaginary
   escape of Farquhar, which actually takes place in a few seconds, pages and pages.
   The time order in this story is not chronological but anachronic, because in the first
   part the whole story is told while the second part suddenly describes the prehistory
   and in the third part the whole story is told again but in a totally different way with
   different experiences. That means that part II is itself a flashback because we learn
   about the prehistory. The reader experiences another flashback in part I in paragraph three when the plot is briefly interrupted by the introduction of Farquhar.

Universität Potsdam

Institut für Anglistik/Amerikanistik

Midterm Assignment

Wintersemester 2010/2011

Abgabe bis: 27.01.2012

Lea Lorena Jerns

05.01.2012

There is also a flash forward right at the beginning of part III that ends before the last sentence. The reader experiences up from the beginning immediately the imaginary escape of Farquhar without knowing why all this is happening and especially what happened before. Another flash forward happens in part I right in the beginning of the story when the reader does not know why this man is on that bridge and is going to be hanged.

Time in terms of history is also important, because this is the real time and enables the reader to put the setting and plot within a specific point of historical time, which is the time of the American Civil War in this case, in order.

5. The story exemplifies the theme of delusion in two different ways. On the one hand there is a delusion with regard to the plot itself, because the main character Farquhar is taken by the false gray-clad soldier and due to this delusion he has to die. On the other hand there is the delusion with regard to the reader, because the reader believes in part III until the unexpected ending that Farquhar has survived. So the narrator plays with the reader with the help of the mixture of story time and discourse time, as well as all these flashbacks and flash forwards mentioned above and finally with the help of the unexpected changes of the narrative perspectives. The combination of all these aspects creates a great delusion that makes it almost impossible for the reader to distinguish between reality and illusion.

Works Cited: Meyer, Michael. *English and American Literatures.*4th ed. Tübingen: Narr Francke Attempto Verlag GmbH + Co.KG, 2011. Print.